HIGHLIGHTS OF AUSTRALASIAN CATHEDRALS

PAUL SCOTT

INTRODUCTION

In 2012, a change in personal circumstances meant that my wife and I had a new freedom to travel. So I suggested to her that, as a project, I photograph all the cathedrals in Australia, making a detailed photographic website of each. Over the next seven years this came to pass, and it was great fun. We visited all parts of the country and many towns that we would never have otherwise visited. The photographs, together with accompanying text, have appeared in publicly accessible websites under the link
http://paulscottinfo.ipage.com/cathedrals/
In succeeding years we travelled further afield to New Zealand, Europe, Wales and England – all the time photographing cathedrals.

Many people who knew me asked if I planned to publish the website results in book form. I was reluctant to do this. How does one compress many thousands of cathedral photos into a book? However in 2023 I published the book *Highlights of English Cathedrals*. This book has been well received, and this has encouraged me to publish a successor, which is this book.

People with a knowledge of cathedrals will notice several 'extras' here. Thus Christ Church Old Cathedral at St Arnaud was a cathedral 1926 – 1977. SS Peter and Paul's Old Cathedral in Goulburn was a cathedral 1869 – 1969. St Mary's in Auckland was a cathedral 1897 – 1973. And Old St Paul's in Wellington was the pro-cathedral of the Anglican Diocese of Wellington 1866 – 1964. All worth including here!

Credits
Front cover, contents page and back cover photos by the author show the Cathedral of the Holy Spirit in Palmerston North, New Zealand, St Michael's Cathedral, Wagga Wagga and St Patrick's Cathedral, Melbourne respectively. The minimal text is factual and heavily dependent on Wikipedia. Nearly all the photographs here are mine. I gratefully acknowledge the few exceptions accredited in the text, used with permission.

About the author …
Paul Scott is a retired mathematics professor from the University of Adelaide, Australia, and a member of St Peter's Anglican Cathedral in Adelaide. His interests have included mathematics education, geometric models, playing in brass bands, photography, construction of websites, churches and cathedrals, volcanoes, light houses, windmills...

Email: paulscott.info@me.com
Web: http://paulscott.info
Flickr: https://www.flickr.com/photos/paulscottinfo/albums/

Copyright © 2023. All rights reserved. No portion of this publication may be used, reproduced or transmitted by any means, digital, electronic, mechanical, photocopy or recording without permission of the publisher, except for the case of brief quotations within critical article or reviews.

ISBN: 978-0-6457817-2-4 (paperback)
ISBN: 978-0-6457817-3-1 (hardcover)

CONTENTS

AUSTRALIA

4 Adelaide	6 Adelaide RC	8 Armidale	10 Armidale RC
12 Ballarat	14 Ballarat RC	16 Bathurst	18 Bathurst RC
20 Bendigo	22 Bendigo RC	24 Brisbane	26 Brisbane RC
28 Broken Hill RC	30 Bunbury	32 Bunbury RC	34 Cairns RC
36 Canberra RC	38 Darwin	40 Darwin RC	42 Geraldton
44 Geraldton RC	46 Goulburn	48 Goulburn RC	50 Grafton
52 Griffith	54 Hobart	56 Hobart RC	58 Lismore RC
60 Melbourne	62 Melbourne RC	64 Murray Bridge	66 Newcastle
68 Newcastle RC	70 Parramatta	72 Parramatta RC	74 Perth
76 Perth RC	78 Port Pirie	80 Port Pirie RC	82 Rockhampton
84 Rockhampton RC	86 Sale	88 Sale RC	90 St Arnaud
92 Sydney	94 Sydney RC	96 Toowoomba RC	98 Townsville
100 Townsville RC	102 Wagga Wagga RC	104 Waitara RC	106 Wangaratta
108 Wollongong RC			

NEW ZEALAND

110 Auckland St M	112 Auckland	114 Auckland RC	116 Christchurch
118 Christchurch RC	120 Dunedin	122 Dunedin RC	124 Hamilton
126 Hamilton RC	128 Napier	130 Nelson	132 New Plymouth
134 Palmerston N RC	136 Wellington Old St P	138 Wellington	140 Wellington RC

◀ Reredos   Peace Chapel   CP Hall window ▶

St Peter's Cathedral is the seat of the Anglican Archbishop of Adelaide. The Cathedral is Gothic in style and dates from 1876. The carved oak reredos is a feature of the Cathedral, and there are some significant stained glass windows. The bells in the Northwest tower are rung every Sunday.

North nave windows

Memorial Garden

Magdalene Window

ADELAIDE RC

St Mary of the Cross

St Francis Xavier Cathedral is the mother church of the Catholic Archdiocese of Adelaide. It is located in the centre of Adelaide, near Victoria Square. The foundation stone was laid in 1856, but the Cathedral was not completed until 1996. The building is classified as being Gothic Revival in Early English style. The tower has 14 bells hung for change ringing.

East window

The Virgin Mary

Nave looking West

Joseph with the boy Jesus

West door panels

ARMIDALE

Flickr : Kerry Myers

◀ One flying buttress!   Tower room museum   Pulpit

St Peter's Cathedral is the mother church of the Anglican Diocese of Armidale, NSW. It was designed by John Horbury Hunt and Bishop James Francis Turner and built 1871 – 1938. The two worked to jointly design a cathedral unlike any Gothic building in Australia. It is fascinatingly different!

Interior arches   South aisle windows   Sanctuary tiling

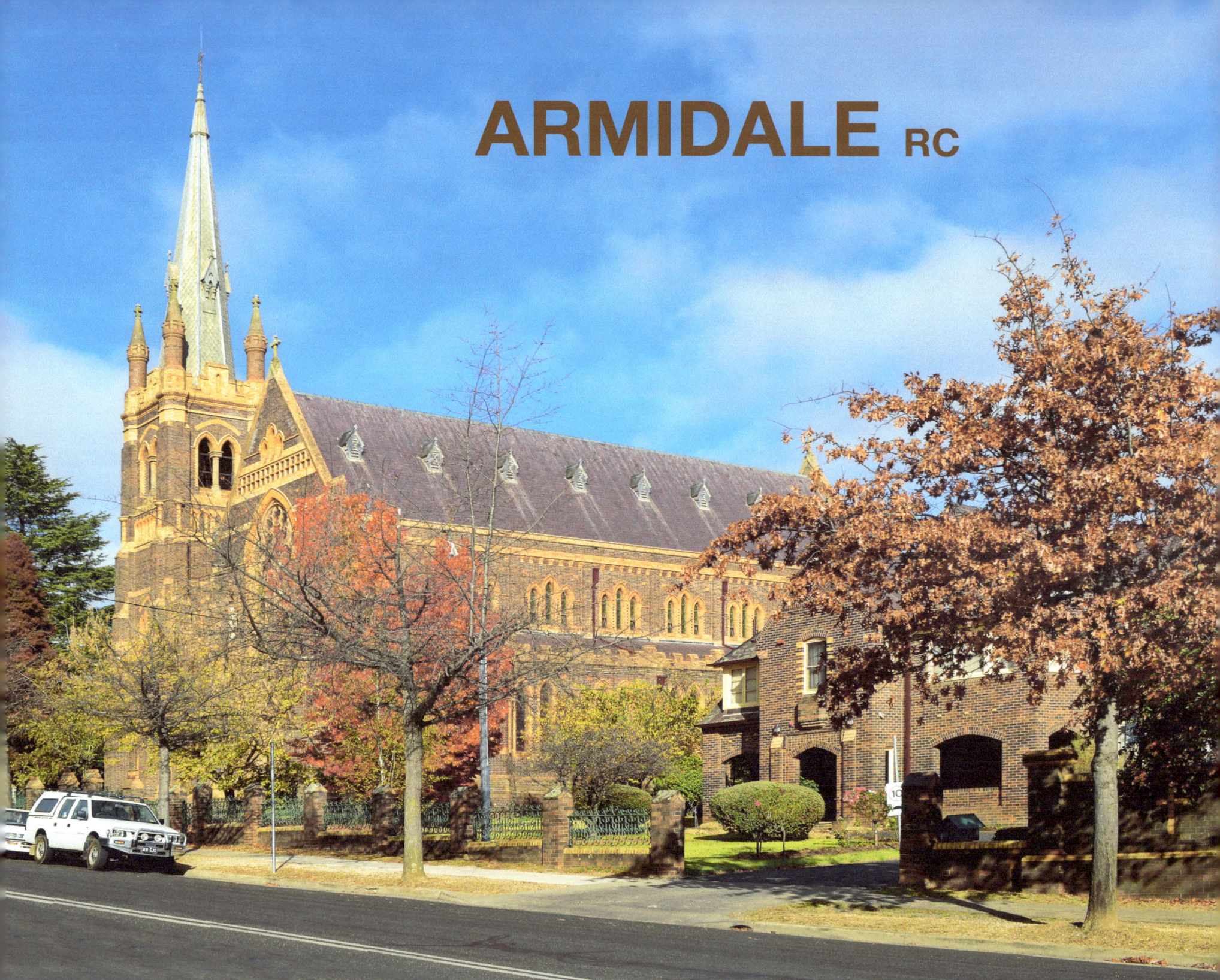

ARMIDALE RC

Built in 1912 in the Federation Gothic Revival style, St Mary & St Joseph Catholic Cathedral is a grand and impressive feature in the Armidale townscape. It is the seat of the Catholic Bishop of Armidale. The building is simple in style but finely detailed, and constructed of Armidale Blue brickwork.

Baptistry

Nave

Organ

Red cedar roof

Font

Lady Chapel

West window

BALLARAT

Lady Chapel windows

Cathedra

Cathedral banner

Carved figure

West window

Stoup

The diocesan cathedral in Ballarat is the Cathedral of Christ the King. The diocese dates from 1875. The present cruciform-shaped Cathedral building evolved over the years from the original Christ Church, amidst unfulfilled dreams as far back as 1886 of building 'a fine new Cathedral'. The present building contains some fine panelling and a number of very fine stained glass windows.

Lectern

BALLARAT RC

Nave

Station of Cross

St Mary McKillop

St Patrick's Cathedral was consecrated in 1891 – the oldest Catholic Cathedral in the Australian colonies. The Church itself is Early Gothic in design and dates from 1858. The high altar and stations of the cross came from Rome. The stained glass windows date from 1883. Five of Ballarat's seven bishops are buried in the crypt.

Nave altar

High altar

East window

Aisle tiling

15

BATHURST

Aisle cross

The cathedral church of the Anglican diocese of Bathurst is All Saints' Cathedral. The original 1845 building was extended / replaced in 1971 by a new nave and bell tower. The combination of old and new works well, and the visitor is in for many surprises!

▶ Nave   Warrior Chapel

Warrior Chapel windows

Modern Christ figure

Font

Entry to nave

Narthex windows

Joseph and Jesus

Nave

The Cathedral of St Michael and St John the Baptist is the seat of the Roman Catholic Bishop of Bathurst. The Cathedral was opened in 1861. Inside, there are a number of interesting features – an example is the nave altar.

Angels

Dramatic nave altar

Jesus and St Francis of Assisi

BENDIGO

Nave with amazing roof

Mosaic reredos

St Paul's Cathedral is the Anglican cathedral of the Diocese of Bendigo. The building is of red brick in an early Gothic style, and is cruciform in shape. It has had structural problems, but some of its beautiful features are shown here.

East window

Rose window

Pipe organ

Christ the King

Ornate crucifix

BENDIGO RC

Northwest view

Nave

Christ icon

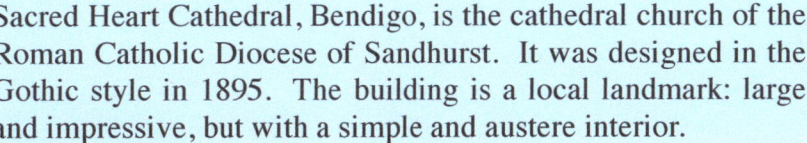
Sacred Heart Cathedral, Bendigo, is the cathedral church of the Roman Catholic Diocese of Sandhurst. It was designed in the Gothic style in 1895. The building is a local landmark: large and impressive, but with a simple and austere interior.

Bernadette of Lourdes

Font

Crucifixion scene

Cathedra

Carved choir canopy
◀◀ Lady Chapel reredos panels ▶▶
◀ Holy Spirit Chapel cross

St John's is the Cathedral of the Anglican Diocese of Brisbane, Queensland. It is the only stone-vaulted church in the Southern Hemisphere, and is an outstanding example of neo-gothic architecture.

North transept rose window   Nave   Lady Chapel appliqué

25

Nave

Old altar panel: the Emmaus story

St Stephen's is the cathedral church of the Roman Catholic Archdiocese of Brisbane. It is a cruciform shaped Gothic Revival cathedral with many striking features such as the spire topped sandstone towers, imported stained glass windows from Munich, the organ, and the newer Blessed Sacrament Chapel.

Above the South nave door

West window

St Joseph with Jesus

Mary woman of faith

Blessed Sacrament Chapel

BROKEN HILL RC

Nave

Sacred Heart Cathedral, Broken Hill is the cathedral church of the Roman Catholic Diocese of Wilcannia-Forbes. It was opened and consecrated in 1905, and is built of stone from the nearby silver mines.

Mosaics behind the Sacred Heart altar

Baptistry

Narthex windows

Lady Chapel reredos

High altar

BUNBURY

Chapel East windows

Nave

St Boniface is the cathedral church of the Anglican Diocese of Bunbury in West Australia. The building is of a modernist brick style and was consecrated in 1962.

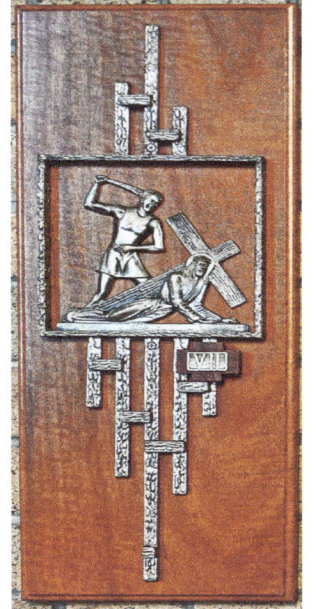
Station of Cross

Christ icon

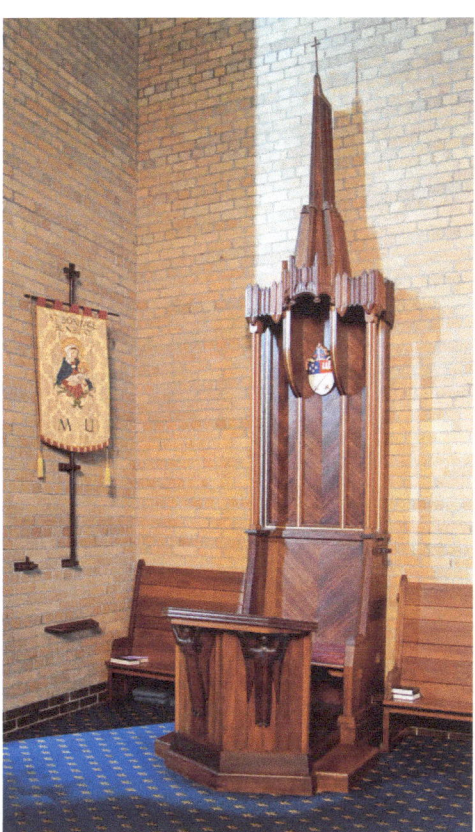
Cathedra

St Boniface legend : West window

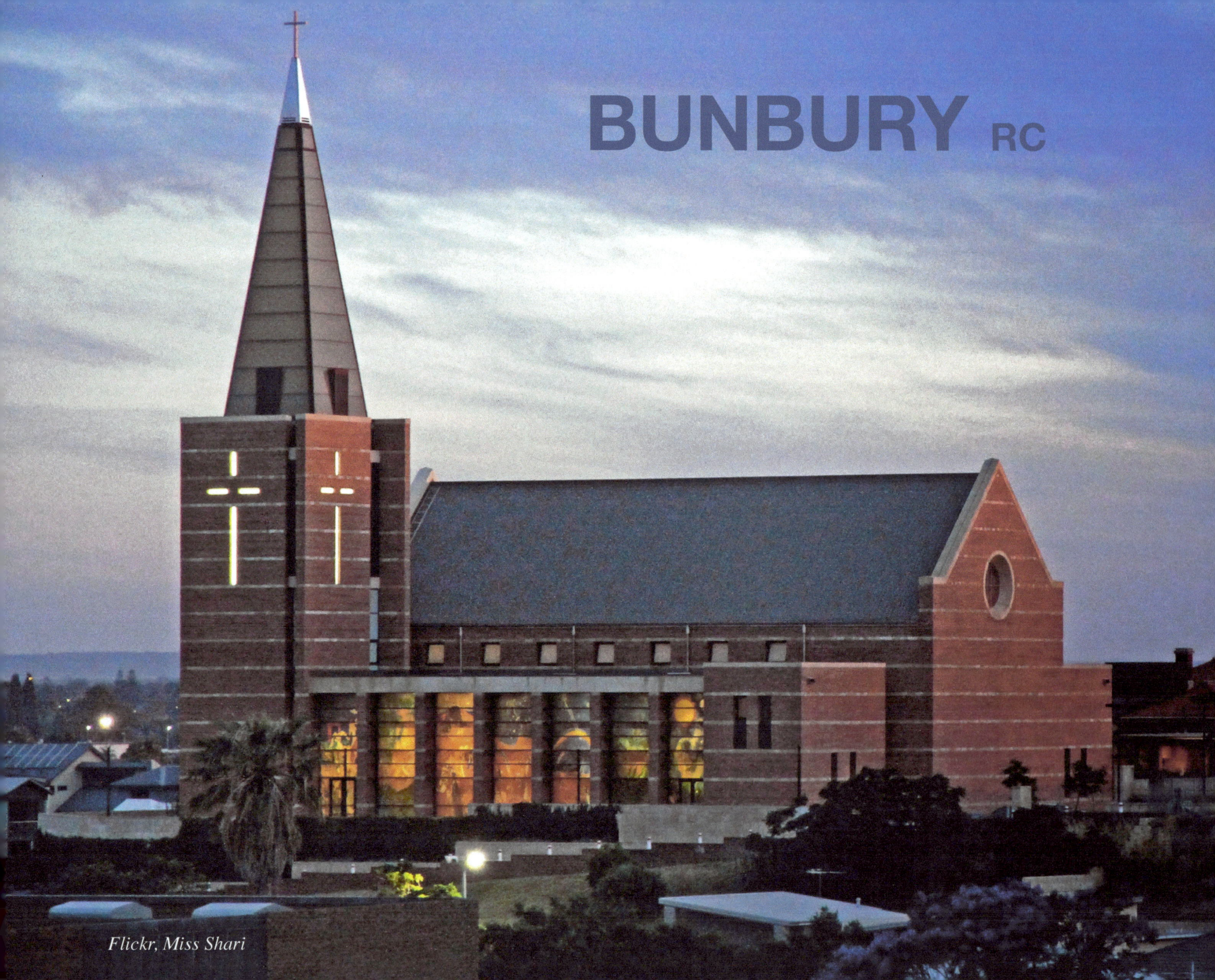
Flickr, Miss Shari

West window

Lady Chapel icon

St Patrick

East window

St Patrick's Catholic Cathedral in Bunbury, West Australia is the seat of the Bishop of the Diocese of Bunbury. This is a new building of modern design, dating from 2011, after a tornado in 2005 severely damaged the existing Cathedral.

Stations of the Cross

Central nave

Narthex window

Panel in one of the nave window walls

CAIRNS RC

St Monica's is the cathedral church of the Catholic Diocese of Cairns. Built 1967–68 in a simple rectangle shape, it is most memorable for its amazing windows. It is a War Memorial Cathedral.

Cyclic from top left: North nave, Paschal candle, sanctuary, baptistry, South nave windows in the Creation series by Jill Stehn.

CANBERRA RC

WA Burdett at English Wikipedia

Nave

▶ Bas-relief of Virgin Mary   Bishop's sacristy
◀ St Christopher and Christ Child

The Roman Catholic Cathedral of St Christopher in Canberra is the seat of the Archbishop of Canberra and Goulburn. The building dates from 1927; it became a pro-Cathedral in 1948, and a full Cathedral in 1973. St Christopher was selected as patron saint because Canberra would be a place to which many travellers would come.

North nave windows

Cathedra

Stations of the Cross

Nave

Memorial window

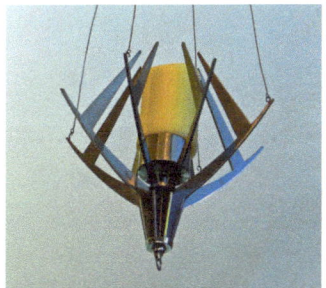
Sanctuary lamp

Christ Church Anglican Cathedral first became a cathedral in 1968 when the Anglican Diocese of the Northern Territory was established in 1968 out of the larger Diocese of Carpentaria, which covered the Northern Territory, North Queensland, and the Tiwi Islands. It was the largest diocese in the world. The Northern Territory Diocese is 'the youngest of the 23 dioceses (regions) of the Anglican Church of Australia'. The building was almost totally destroyed by Cyclone Tracy in 1974.

Annunciation

Baptism of Jesus

Crucifix

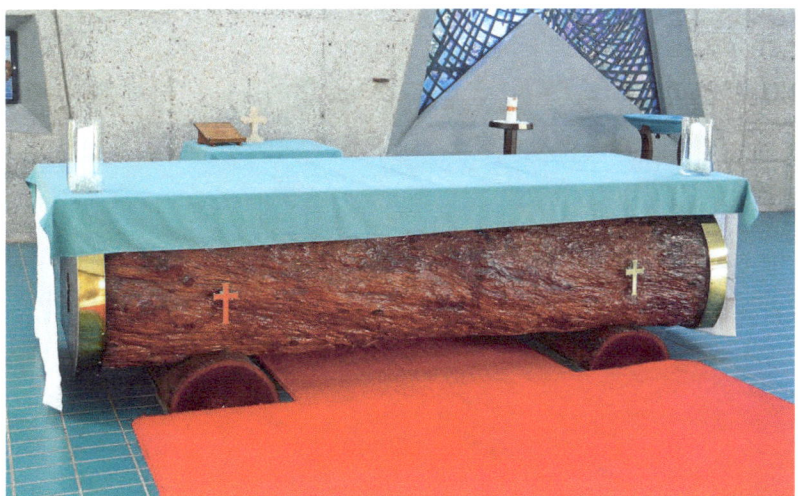
Nave altar

DARWIN RC

Disfigured crucifix

West wall

Memorial panels

Front altar panel

The St Mary's Star of the Sea Cathedral is the seat of the bishop of the Diocese of Darwin. The Cathedral was blessed and opened in 1962. Its unusual parabolic design has proved to be resistant to cyclones. It has many unusual features, some of which are illustrated here.

Parabolic nave

Aboriginal Madonna and Child

Wounded angel

ANGLICAN CHURCH OF AUSTRALIA
THE CATHEDRAL OF THE HOLY CROSS
SUNDAY CHURCH 6.45AM 8.15AM 10.00AM
WEDNESDAY CHURCH 10.00AM

GERALDTON

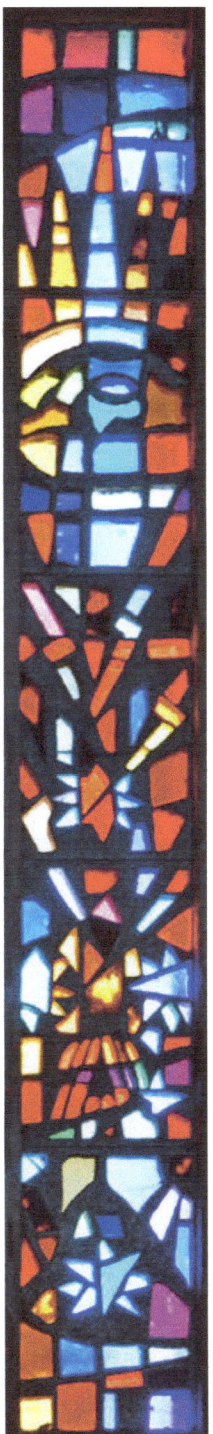

◀ Bishop's crest   Nave   Altar support   Lectern ▶

The first service in Geraldton's Anglican Cathedral of the Holy Cross was held in 1964. The building has been described as one of the finest examples of modern brutalist architecture in Australia – forbidding walls, exposed concrete, monochrome palette … . Like its environs: rugged, bold, strong.

Nave window   Cathedra   Creation window   Madonna and Child   Nave window   43

Western towers

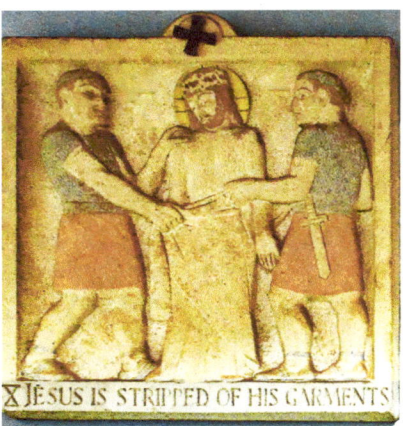
Station of Cross

St Joseph and Jesus

Crossing window: St Mark

Transept window: the Nativity

St. Francis Xavier's Cathedral is a Roman Catholic cathedral in Geraldton, Western Australia. It is the seat of the Bishop of Geraldton. It was opened in 1938, and is the largest and most imposing work of priest and architect John Hawes. The building is unusual and spectacular, inside and out.

Crossing window: St John

St Peter with shiny boot!

Nave

45

GOULBURN

Roof   Archangel Michael   Nave

◀ Nativity roundels : shepherds and wise men ▶

St Saviour's Cathedral is the heritage-listed cathedral church of the Anglican Diocese of Canberra and Goulburn in Goulburn, New South Wales. It was founded in 1874 and designed by noted architect Edmund Blacket. The cathedral was Blacket's favourite building and is a delight to visit. It is interesting that St Saviour's is located in Goulburn while the diocesan bishop and the diocesan office are located in Canberra, the nation's capital, 87 kilometres to the south of Goulburn.

Madonna and Child icon   Pelican tile   West wall hanging   Font

GOULBURN RC

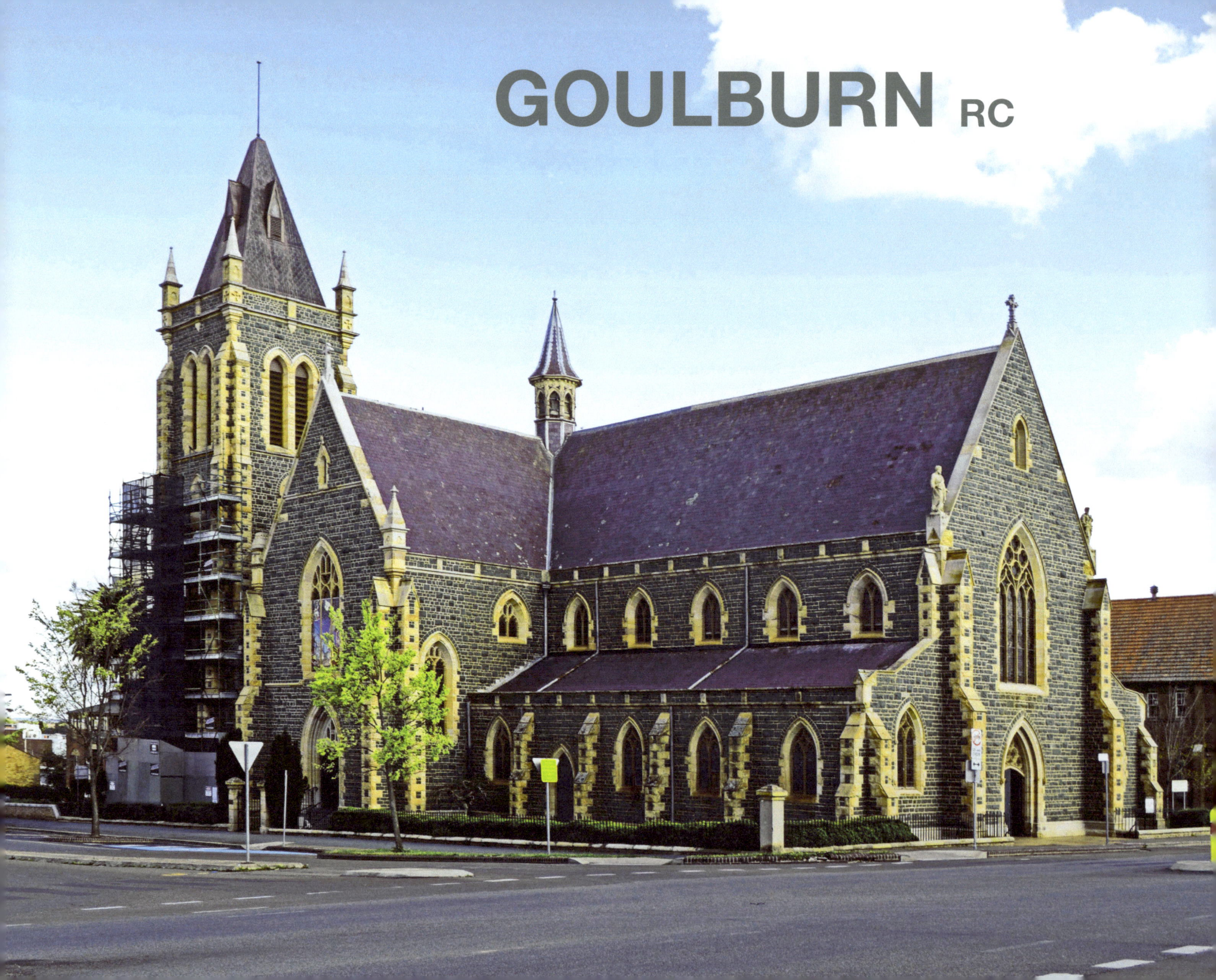

Tower detail

West window

Good Shepherd screen

High altar

St Peter and Paul's Old Cathedral is a former Catholic cathedral in Goulburn, New South Wales. The diocesan centre was transferred to Canberra in 1969. This is an unusual greenstone building which was opened in 1873. It is a lovely old church but was sadly suffering from salt damp and neglect when I visited in 2015.

Organ

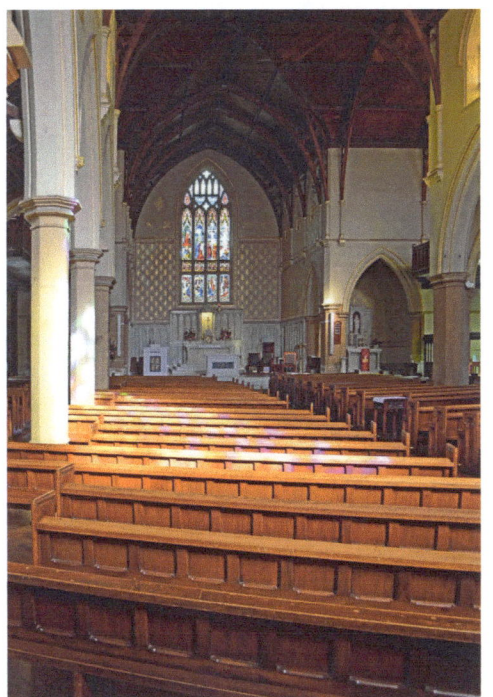
Nave

North entry mosaic

Sword and cross-keys logo

GRAFTON

▼ Baptistry windows   ▲ Nave windows

Stations of the Cross

Christ Church Cathedral is a heritage-listed Anglican cathedral in Grafton, New South Wales. It is also known as the Cathedral Church of Christ the King. The cathedral was designed by John Horbury Hunt and built from 1874 to 1884. The cathedral seats 1000 people. There is a touching story of a little girl who gave her doll towards the initial building of the cathedral. The doll can still be seen high in the West wall.

Nave

Aisle floor tiles

The Story of the Doll

The doll in this cabinet is a twin of the one in the brickwork above the Great West Doors. The doll is between two bricks in the arch over the central window in the western porch. The doll was placed in the temporary west wall in 1883. When the wall was demolished for the Cathedral extension in 1937, it was carefully removed, treated with preservative and placed in the new west wall where it can be seen today.

The dolls belonged to Bella and May Greenaway. One of the girls gave her doll to be set into the wall. The other doll remained in the family and was given to the Cathedral in 1984 by Marie Cains, who is a direct descendant of the Greenaway family.

Story of two girls and their dolls

GRIFFITH

St Christopher window

Cathedra

Time for prayer

To the nave

Triptych

St Alban's Cathedral in Griffith, New South Wales, is the cathedral of the Riverina diocese. The foundation stone for the present building was laid in 1954. The building became the cathedral in 1984 as part of the diocese's centenary celebrations.

Stations of the Cross

Altar Cross

St Anne with child Mary
◀ West Nativity window

The Cathedral Church of St David in Hobart is the seat of the Anglican Bishop of Tasmania. The foundation stone of the cathedral was laid in 1868 by Prince Alfred, Duke of Edinburgh, a son of Queen Victoria, and it was built between then and 1936, in the Gothic Revival style. The Cathedral's distinctive features include an arcaded entrance with a large West window and buttressed turrets; a square tower made of Oatlands stone; and a close on the southern side with old trees.

Mothers' Union banner

Antarctic sledge flag

Nave parquetry floor

Nave

Choir screen

HOBART RC

Unusual nave windows featuring Mary

◀ Quatrefoil   Tapestry: Lady of Perpetual Help ▶

St Mary's Cathedral in Hobart, Tasmania, Australia, is the seat of the Roman Catholic Archbishop of Hobart. The cathedral was built in the Gothic Revival style and was consecrated in 1866. Major reconstruction took place later. The windows are a special feature of St Mary's.

Nave altar

Nave

Sacred Heart Chapel Altar

LISMORE RC

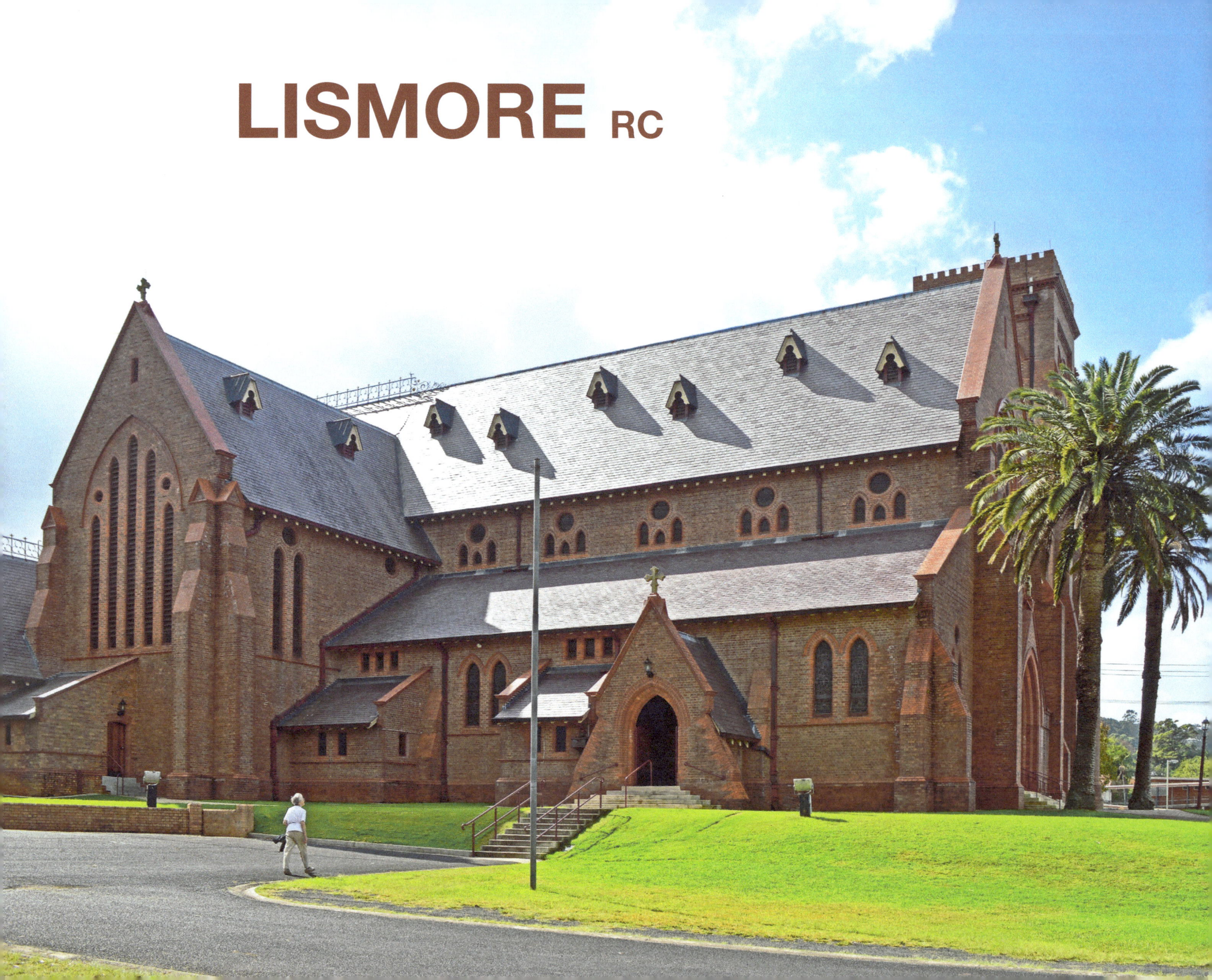

Round West window

Candlestick

Cathedra

St Patrick shrine

St Carthage's Cathedral, Lismore is the seat of the Roman Catholic Bishop of Lismore. The diocese was created in 1887 and the Cathedral dates from 1907, its building largely due to the efforts of Bishop Jeremiah Doyle. The Cathedral was damaged by flooding in 2022.

Nave

Rood Cross

Front ambo panel

Memorial plaque

Lantern Window

Processional doors

Nave tiling

St Paul's Cathedral in Melbourne, Victoria is the cathedral church of the Anglican Diocese of Melbourne. It is built on the site where the first public Christian service in Melbourne was conducted in 1835. Designed by William Butterfield, it was built in Gothic Revival style and consecrated in 1891. The spires were added later and completed in 1933. The interior features rich colours and strident colour contrasts.

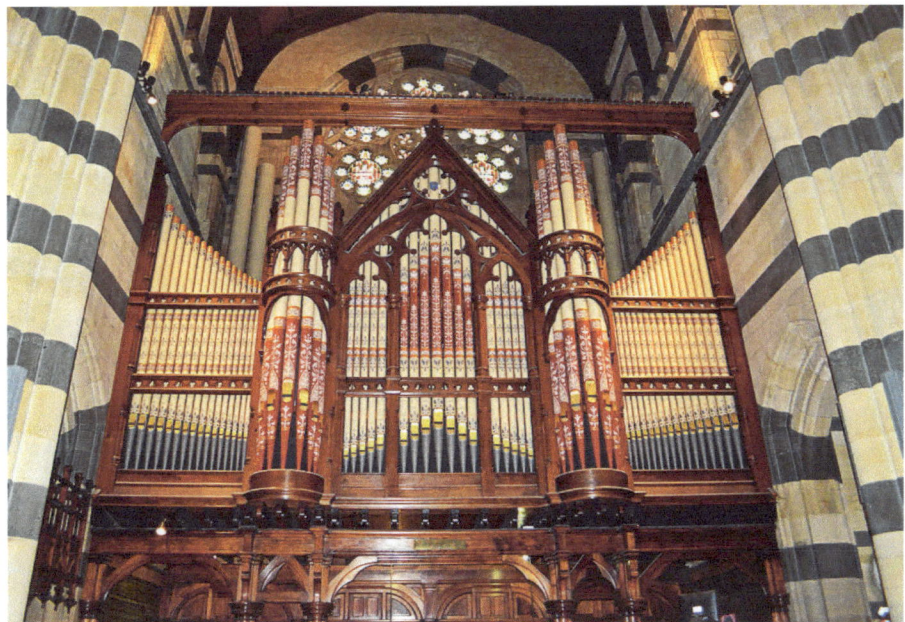
South transept Lewis organ

Sanctuary reredos

Archbishop's cathedra

61

MELBOURNE RC

Southwest view

Baptismal font

Candle stand

West window

St Patrick's Cathedral is the cathedral church of the Roman Catholic Archdiocese of Melbourne in Victoria, and seat of its archbishop. In 1974 Pope Paul VI conferred the title and dignity of minor basilica on it. Built in the style of a Latin cross, St Patrick's has the distinction of being both the tallest and, overall, the largest church building in Australia. It was dedicated in 1851 and consecrated in 1897.

Lady Chapel railing

Southern water feature

Nave

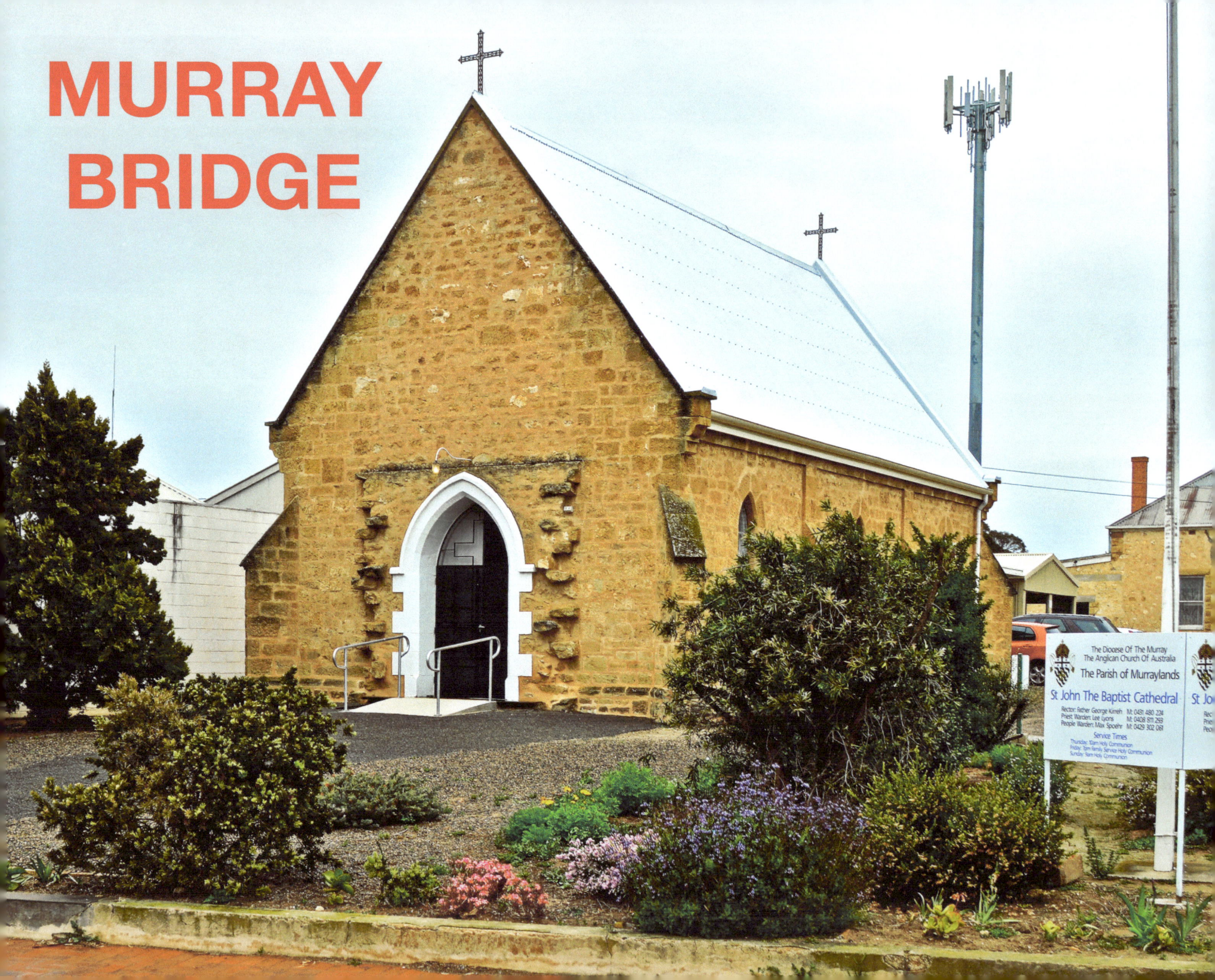

Cathedral sign board

St John the Baptist Cathedral, Murray Bridge, is the cathedral church of the Anglican Diocese of The Murray, South Australia, which covers 52,426 square kilometres. The original church was built of rough stone as a parish church in 1887, and with a maximum seating capacity of 130, is the smallest cathedral in Australia. The interior of the cathedral is decorated in the High Church tradition.

Stations of the Cross

Sanctuary window

Nave

Cathedra

Kneeler

Sanctuary window

Old bell tower

Baptismal font

The Cathedral Church of Christ the King, also called Christ Church Cathedral, is a cathedral in Newcastle, New South Wales. It is the cathedral church of the Diocese of Newcastle in the Anglican Church of Australia. The building, designed by John Horbury Hunt in the Gothic Revival style was consecrated in 1983. It is located on a hill at the city's eastern end in the suburb called The Hill. It suffered bad damage in the 1989 earthquake. This cathedral has many items of interest, and is definitely worth a visit!

Nave

Last Supper : sanctuary reredos panel

St Christopher Chapel with 'Chippy'

Burne-Jones window

Four Evangelist wands

NEWCASTLE RC

Mary Alacoque Chapel

Sanctuary

Crucifix

Angel stoup

Rood Cross

Sacred Heart Cathedral is located in Hamilton, a suburb of Newcastle, New South Wales. It is the Catholic cathedral church of the Diocese of Maitland-Newcastle. The foundation stone for the church was laid in 1928, and it took ten months in 1929 to put the 700,000 bricks in place. The Church of the Sacred Heart was officially opened in 1930 as the parish church of Hamilton. It became the Sacred Heart Cathedral in 1995, along with the creation of the diocese.

Welcoming Jesus

Stations of the Cross

Nave

PARRAMATTA

North nave window

Historic Māori font

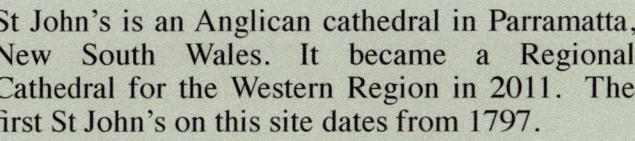
St John's is an Anglican cathedral in Parramatta, New South Wales. It became a Regional Cathedral for the Western Region in 2011. The first St John's on this site dates from 1797.

Clergy stalls

North transept window

Macarthur monument

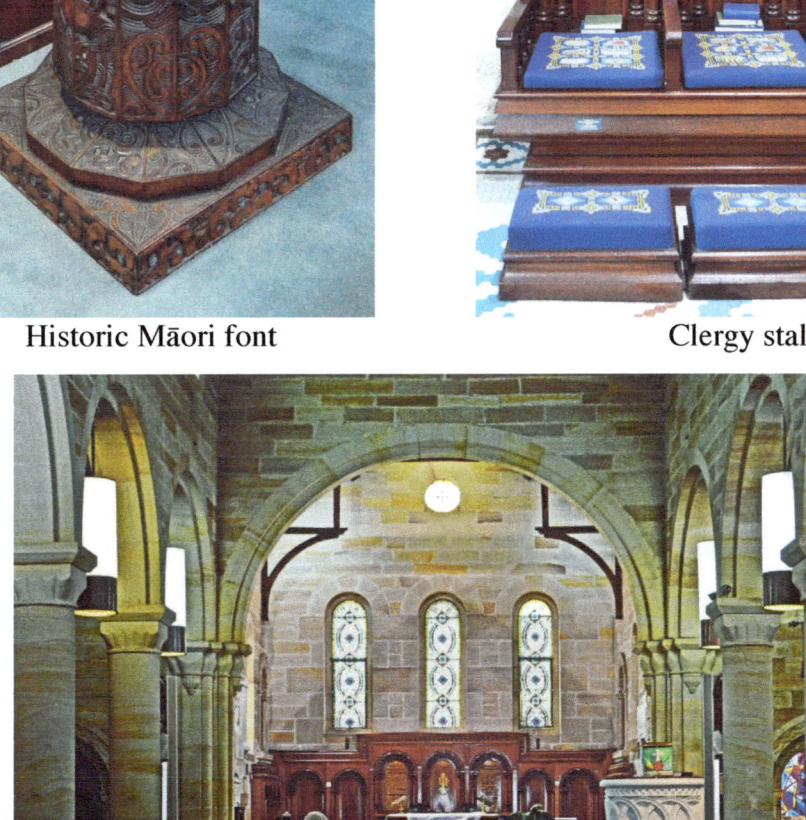
Nave (flower day!)

Bell pulls

PARRAMATTA RC

St Patrick (exterior)

Modern tabernacle (New chapel)

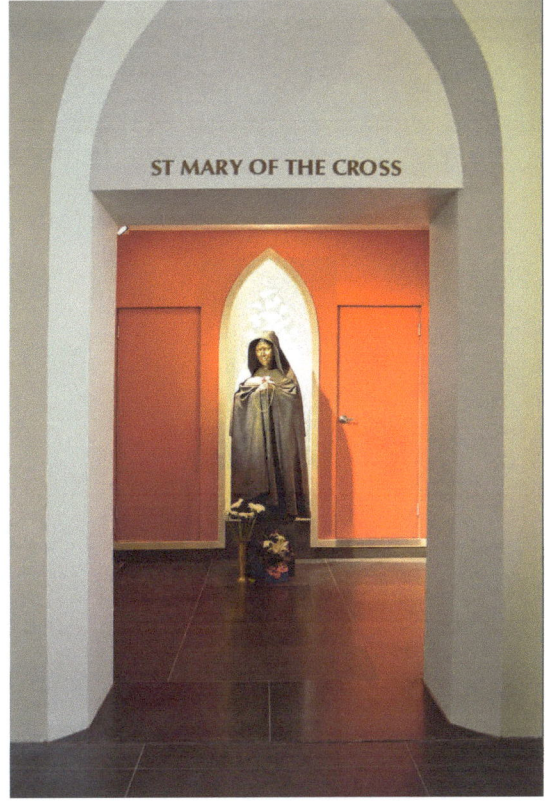
St Mary of the Cross

Tip of spire

St Patrick's Cathedral, Parramatta is the Catholic cathedral church of the Diocese of Parramatta. The original 1854 Church was destroyed by fire in 1996 and rebuilt with the old Church as a chapel and a large auditorium added to one side.

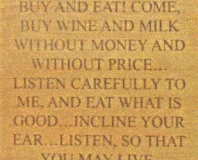 
Modern Station of Cross (auditorium)

Windows (new chapel)

Organ (auditorium)

Ascalon

Remembrance Chapel

Spiral stair to organ

Nave

St George

Christ icon

St George's Cathedral was built 1879–1888. It is the principal Anglican church in the city of Perth, Western Australia. It was designed by the noted Australian architect Edmund Blacket in Victorian Academic Gothic style. The red brick gives it a warm welcoming feel. Ascalon (the sculpture) is the lance used by St George.

Prophets window

Dramatic nave altar figure

PERTH RC

Entry door

St Joseph alcove

Transept window

Tabernacle

Cathedra

St Mary's Cathedral, Perth, Western Australia, officially the Cathedral of the Immaculate Conception of the Blessed Virgin Mary, is the cathedral church of the Roman Catholic Archdiocese of Perth. The cathedral was founded in 1865 and extended in Academic Gothic style from 1926. Further extensions including a second spire and a curved seating area for 1600 people were completed in 2009. St Mary's has a beautiful setting in Victoria Park, just east of central Perth.

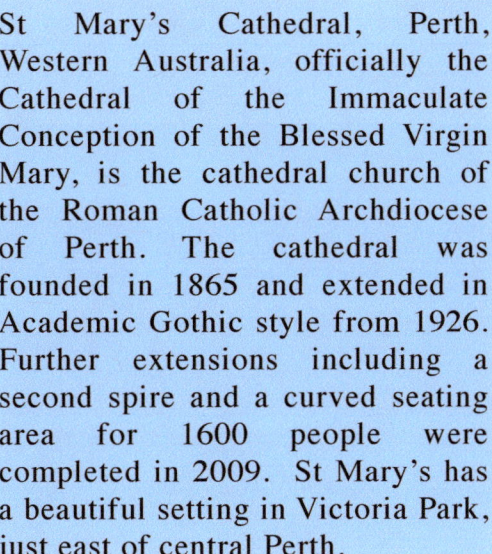
Station of the Cross

Nave

PORT PIRIE

Nave

Crucifix

Cathedra

The Diocese of Willochra was founded in 1915, but it was 84 years later that a Cathedral Church was designated. On 29th June 1999, the feast day of the two patron saints, the Church of Saints Peter & Paul, Port Pirie, South Australia, became the Cathedral Church of this Diocese.

Diocese emblem

Christ window

St Andrew window

Cathedra detail

Altar cross

PORT PIRIE RC

Nave

Station of the Cross

St Mark's is the Roman Catholic Cathedral in the city of Port Pirie, South Australia. The church was founded in 1882, and became a cathedral in 1887. It was destroyed by fire in 1947. The newly restored cathedral was reopened in 1953.

Sanctuary window   Modern lectern   Tabernacle   Paschal candle   Sanctuary window

Northwest view

South wall

Bell tower

St Paul's Anglican Cathedral was constructed as the parish church in Rockhampton, Queensland, and completed by 1883 when it was dedicated. The building was designed principally by Brisbane architect Annersley Voysey. The building became the Anglican cathedral in 1892. The building was closed in 2017 due to structural problems (the time of my visit!), but is now back in use.

Consecration service

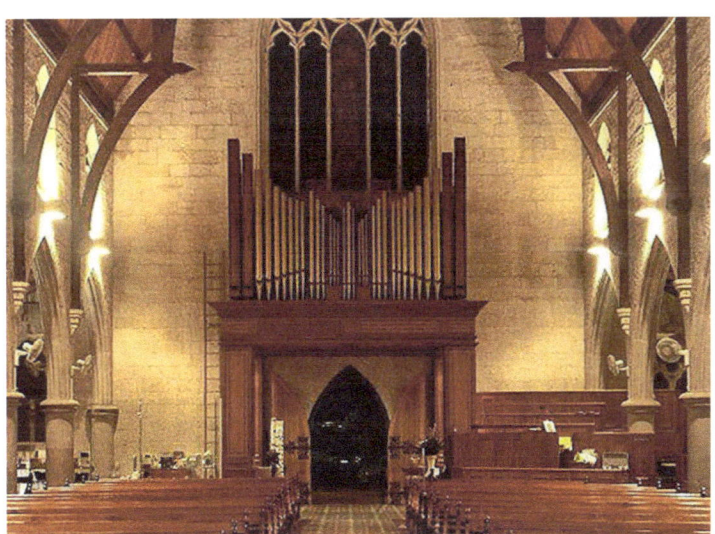
West wall and organ

Nave

ROCKHAMPTON RC

Southwest view

Spacious nave

St Joseph's Cathedral is a heritage-listed Roman Catholic cathedral in Rockhampton, Queensland, Australia. It was designed by Francis Drummond Greville Stanley and built from 1893 to 1982. It is a wonderful cathedral with many items of interest.

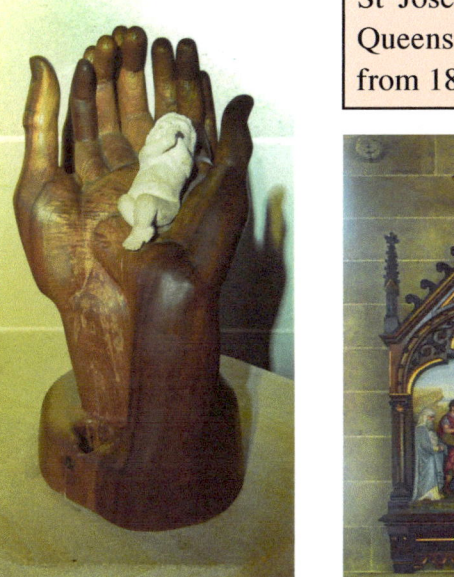
Hands carving

Stations of the Cross

Nave windows

Chapel lamp

85

SALE

Nave windows

Font

Stone collection

Cathedra

Nave windows

Musical organ window

Nave windows

St Paul's in Sale, Victoria is the cathedral church of the Anglican Diocese of Gippsland. It was built in 1884 to a design by Nathaniel Billing, with a rectangular footprint and is constructed of red brick and slate roofing. It became cathedral of the diocese in 1920.

SALE RC

Angel trumpeter

Assembly Area Windows

Nave altar

Our Lady

St Mary's, in the provincial city of Sale, in the East Gippsland region of Victoria, is the Roman Catholic cathedral church of the Diocese of Sale. It was designed in the Gothic Revival style in 1886 by architects, Barker and Henderson, and dedicated in 1910. It has many beautiful features, and is of special interest because of the tastefully added free-form assembly area on the South side of the original church.

Nave windows: Matthew, Mark

Sanctuary

Nave windows: Luke, John

Lydia windows

Nave

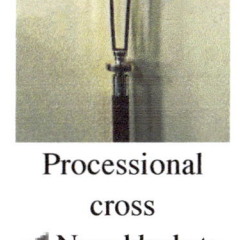
Processional cross
◀ Nave blankets
Church sign ▶
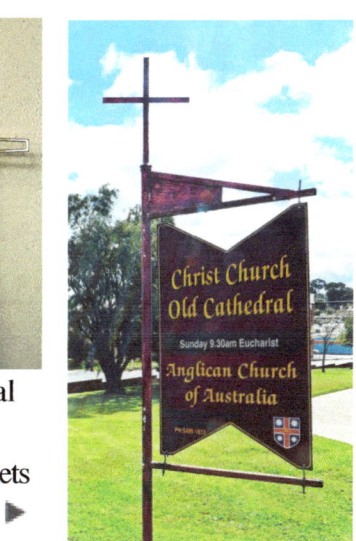

The Anglican Diocese of St Arnaud was a diocese in north-west Victoria. It was created in 1926 out of the Diocese of Ballarat and named after the town of St Arnaud. In 1976 it was amalgamated into the Diocese of Bendigo. The beautiful cathedral church was Christ Church, now known as Christ Church Old Cathedral. It was designed by F. M. Moore and built in 1864 in Early English Gothic style.

Amazing nave roof-line

Metal sculpture

Nave altar

91

Great West window

Chancel tiling

Nave windows

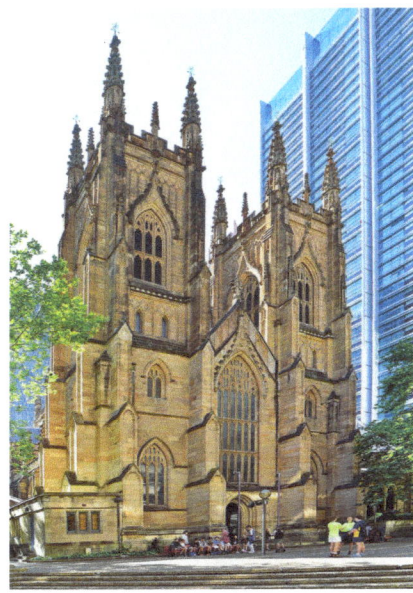

West wall

Nave

Organ

St Andrew's is the cathedral church of the Anglican Diocese of Sydney, New South Wales. Designed primarily by Edmund Blacket on foundations laid by James Hume, the Cathedral was built from 1837 to 1868, and was ready for services and consecrated in 1868, making it the oldest cathedral in Australia. St Andrew's is one of the city's finest examples of Gothic Revival architecture.

Reredos

Virgin Mary and Christ Child

Nave

Pope John Paul

St Anne with Mary

St Mary's Cathedral is the cathedral church of the Roman Catholic Archdiocese of Sydney, New South Wales. It is dedicated to the 'Immaculate Mother of God, Help of Christians', and is a minor basilica. Its architects were William Wardell and Augustus Welby Pugin, and it became a cathedral in 1865. It is the longest church in Australia.

Reredos in Lady Chapel

Detail of window in Chapel of Irish Saints

Baptismal font

Reredos detail

Old bell

Nave

St Patrick's is the cathedral of the Roman Catholic Diocese of Toowoomba, Queensland. It was designed by Toowoomba architect James Marks and was built from 1883 to 1935. It is built in Victoria Gothic style and became a cathedral in 1929.

West window

Stations of the Cross

Nave light

Unusual baptistry

97

Grotto

Rood Cross

Three fish window (top)

St James' is the cathedral church of the Anglican Diocese of North Queensland at Townsville, Queensland. It was designed by Arthur Blacket and was built in 1887 by MacMahon & Cliffe. The Gothic revival building has many interesting features.

West nave mosaic

Gold lamp

Nave windows

Nave

99

TOWNSVILLE RC

Cathedral Photo

Sacred Heart

Conch shells

Nave

Sacred Heart Cathedral is the Roman Catholic Cathedral of Townsville, Queensland. It was built from 1896 to 1902 by Dennis Kelleher. The building was severely damaged by Cyclone Leonta in 1903, just three months after opening. It was repaired, and became a cathedral in 1921. It was completely refurbished in the early 2000s, and has been given many modern touches whilst retaining its beautiful beginnings.

Tower doors

Stations of the Cross

Virgin Mary

Reredos: Annunciation

WAGGA WAGGA RC

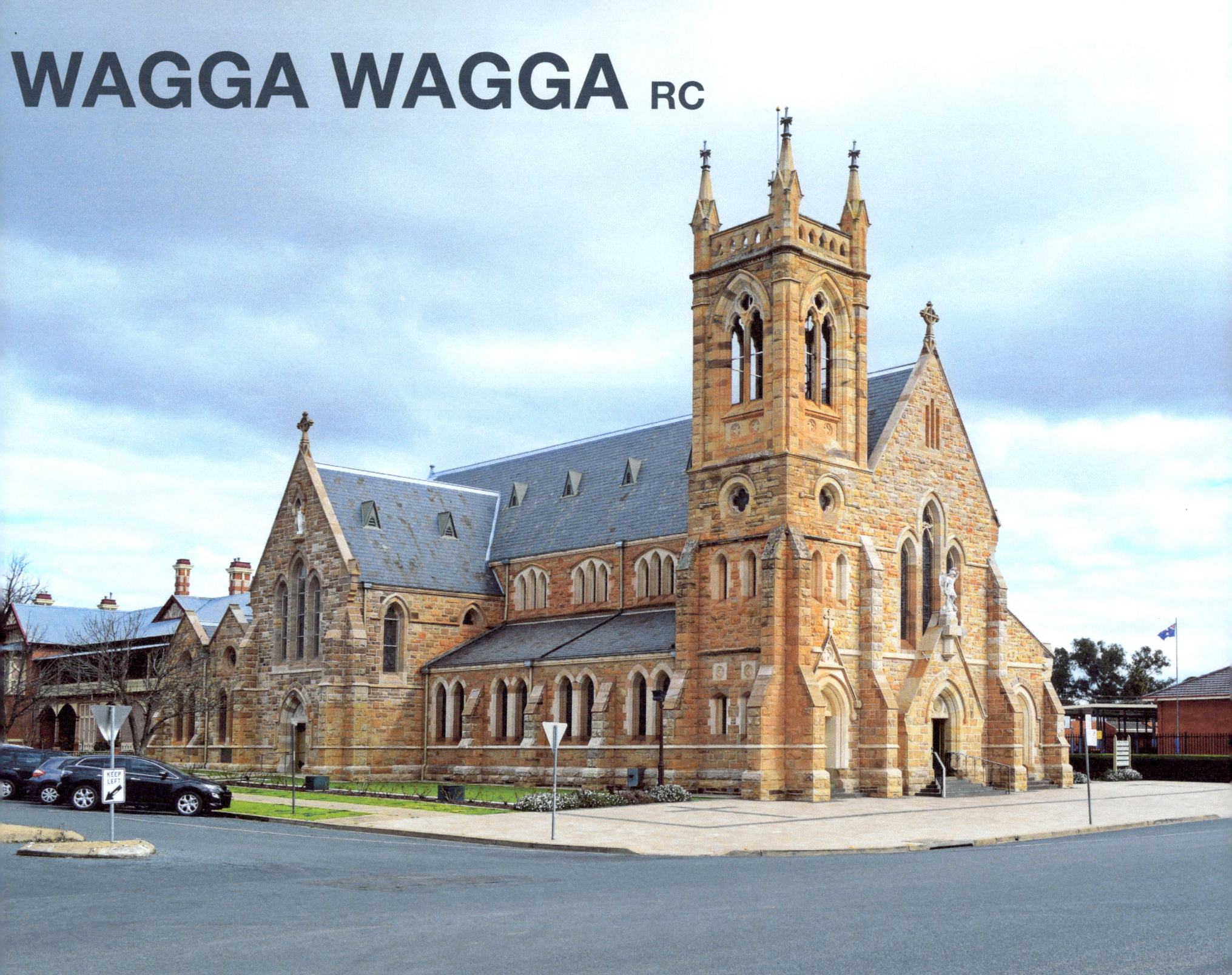

Cathedra crest

St Michael

St Joseph with Jesus

Musical window

St Michael's in Wagga Wagga, New South Wales, is the cathedral church of the Roman Catholic Diocese of Wagga Wagga. The building was competed in 1887, and became a cathedral in 1925.

Nave windows

Transept quatrefoil

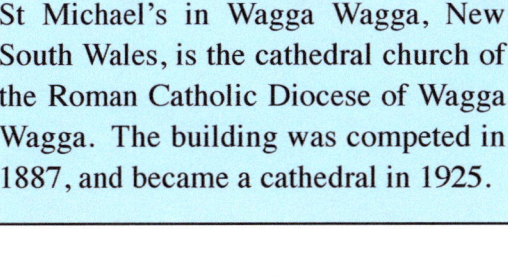

Sanctuary mosaic

Nave

103

Memorial crucifix

Nave

Altar

Waitara is a suburb of Sydney, New South Wales, 19 kilometres north-west of the city. It is here we find Our Lady of the Rosary Cathedral, the cathedral church of the Roman Catholic Diocese of Broken Bay. The Diocese was established in 1986, but it was not until 2008 that Our Lady of the Rosary was designated as the Cathedral of the Diocese.

Virgin Mary with Jesus

Holy oils

Baptismal window

Ambo

Crucifixion window

WANGARATTA

Garden crucifix

Nave windows

Unexpected narthex window

Baptistery

Holy Trinity is the Cathedral Church of the Diocese of Wangaratta, Victoria. The Diocese was founded in 1902; the Cathedral opened in 1909. The baptistery was completed in 1965. The Cathedral houses eight change ringing bells in a long standing temporary tower!

Madonna

Nave

Lady Chapel

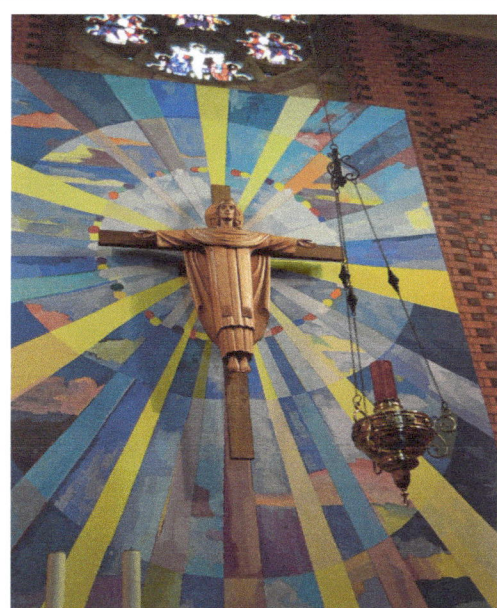
Christ Figure

Baptistery window

WOLLONGONG

Photo Credit: Wikimedia John Armagh

Black Madonna

Nave

Angels

St Francis Xavier Cathedral, in Wollongong, New South Wales, is the seat of the Roman Catholic Bishop of the Diocese of Wollongong. The building is Gothic in style and was completed in 1848, but the interior has been extensively modified since then.

Christ icon

West door

Sanctuary

St Francis Xavier

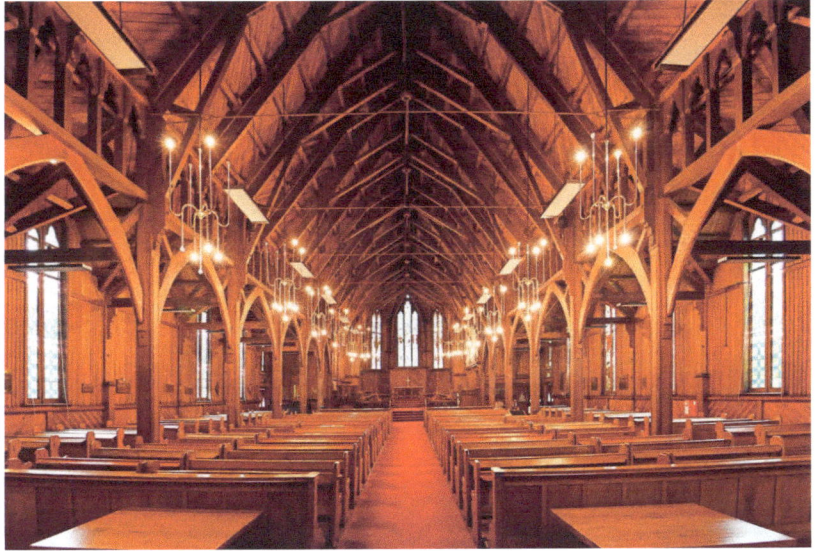
Nave

Pulpit

Lectern

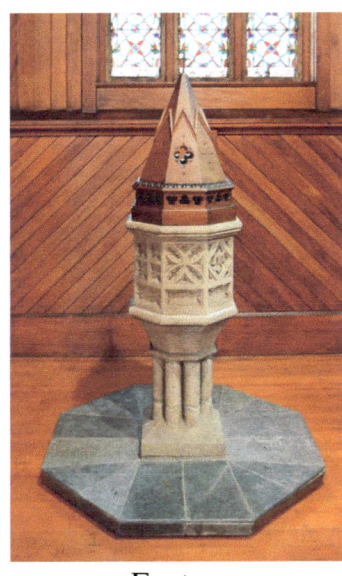
Font

St Mary's Cathedral Church is the former cathedral church of the **Anglican Diocese of Auckland**. It served as cathedral from 1897 to 1973. It is the longest wooden Gothic church in the world, and sits beside the present cathedral.

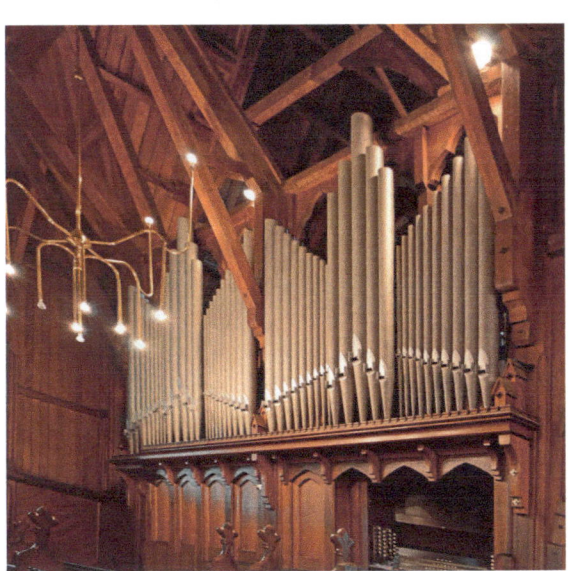
Pipe organ

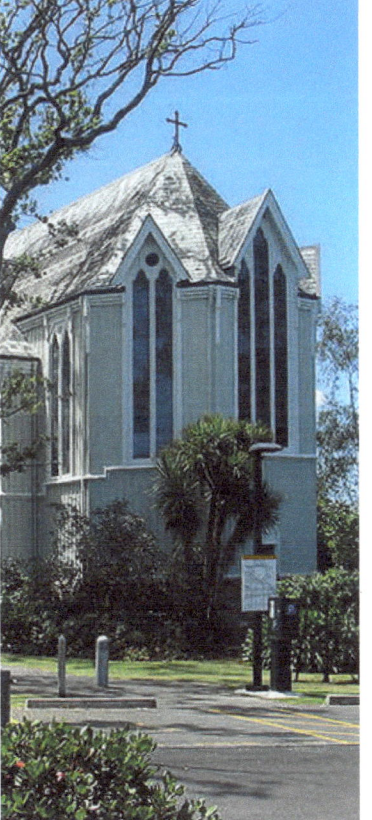
Apse

Sanctuary apse windows

AUCKLAND

Nave

Nave windows

Holy Trinity Cathedral in Auckland, New Zealand is the 'mother church' of the Anglican Diocese of Auckland. The current main church building was consecrated in 1973. It is a building filled with thoughtful creativity and colour.

Paschal candle and font

Round window

Ship's bell

Nave to the West

Jesus Divine Workman

St Vincent de Paul

Nave

Aroha Holy Family sculpture

The Cathedral of St Patrick and St Joseph (usually known as St Patrick's Cathedral) is a **Catholic church in central Auckland**. It is the **mother church of the Roman Catholic Diocese of Auckland**. A wooden chapel was constructed in 1842, replaced by a stone church in 1848 which was expanded in 1884, and finally replaced with the current cathedral in 1907. The church was designated as a cathedral in 1848, and **consecrated** in 1963.

Stations of the Cross

Lord Jesus, you are like the sun in the sky,
The light shining in our darkness
So that we ourselves can become the light.

Lord Jesus, you died in pain on the cross,
You rose again from the dead.
Now you live within us,
You live our lives and die our deaths with us.

Lord Jesus, all that is in heaven belongs to you,
All things that are on earth.
Send your Spirit like a river of clear water
Flowing through our hearts.

Lord Jesus, you are the house and we are the timber,
You are the vine and we are the branches.
Send your Spirit so that the vine may flower,
Heal in us whatever is at fault.

James K. Baxter 1972

Verse by James Baxter

Nave windows

CHRISTCHURCH

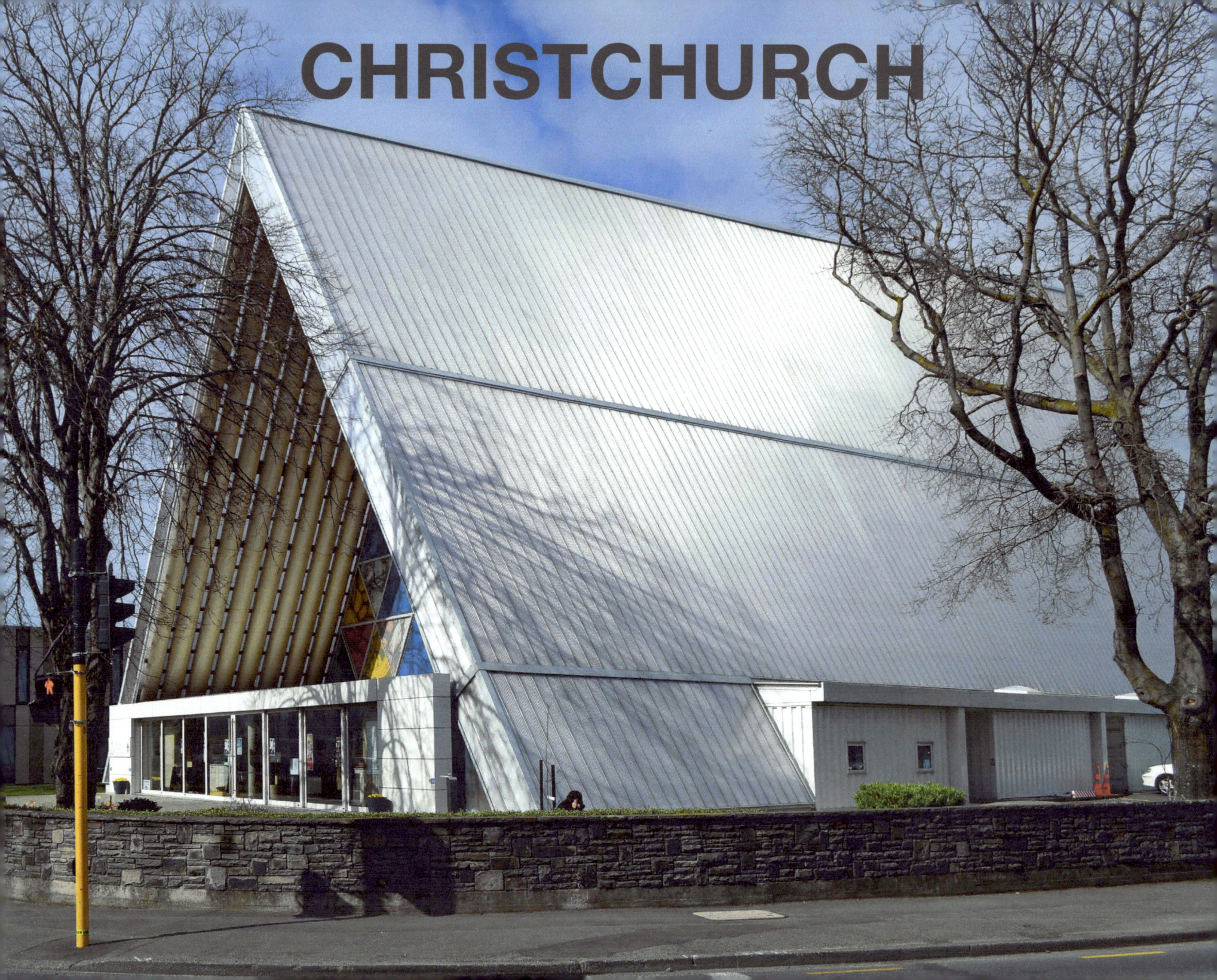

The much loved old Cathedral

Memorial sculpture

Font

New 'Cardboard Cathedral'

Christchurch Cathedral, also called Christ Church Cathedral, is a deconsecrated Anglican cathedral in the city of Christchurch. It was built between 1864 and 1904 in the city centre, surrounded by Cathedral Square. Tragically, it was very badly damaged in the 2011 earthquakes, and since 2013 the congregation has worshipped in the Cardboard Cathedral. Work began in 2019 on reinstating the old Cathedral.

Destruction

Old Cathedral nave

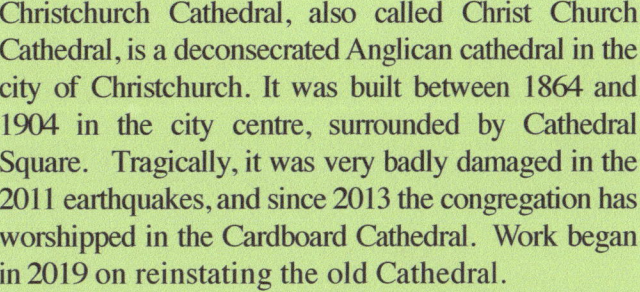
Cardboard Cathedral nave

New East end

CHRISTCHURCH RC

Model Cathedral, Quake City

Grotto

Bell

Interior 2009

The Cathedral of the Blessed Sacrament (Christchurch Basilica) was a Catholic cathedral in **Christchurch**. It was destroyed in the 2010 / 2011 earthquakes, and demolition was completed in 2021. A new Cathedral is due to be completed in 2025 in a new location.

Destruction

West wall

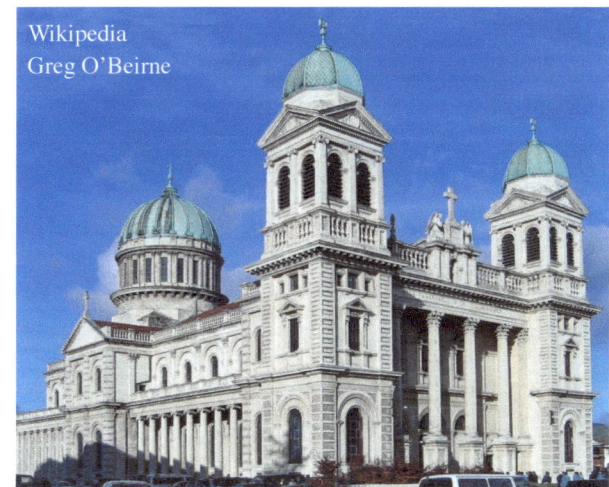
Northwest view 2012

Northwest view

Nave looking towards the new Eastern apse

Western War Memorial Window

Pulpit panel

St Paul's Cathedral is the seat of the Bishop of the Anglican diocese of Dunedin. Building began in 1915, and the Cathedral was consecrated in 1919. A new modern chancel was added in 1971, but was damaged by fire in 2020.

Robinson Porch windows

Māori Cross

Baptismal font

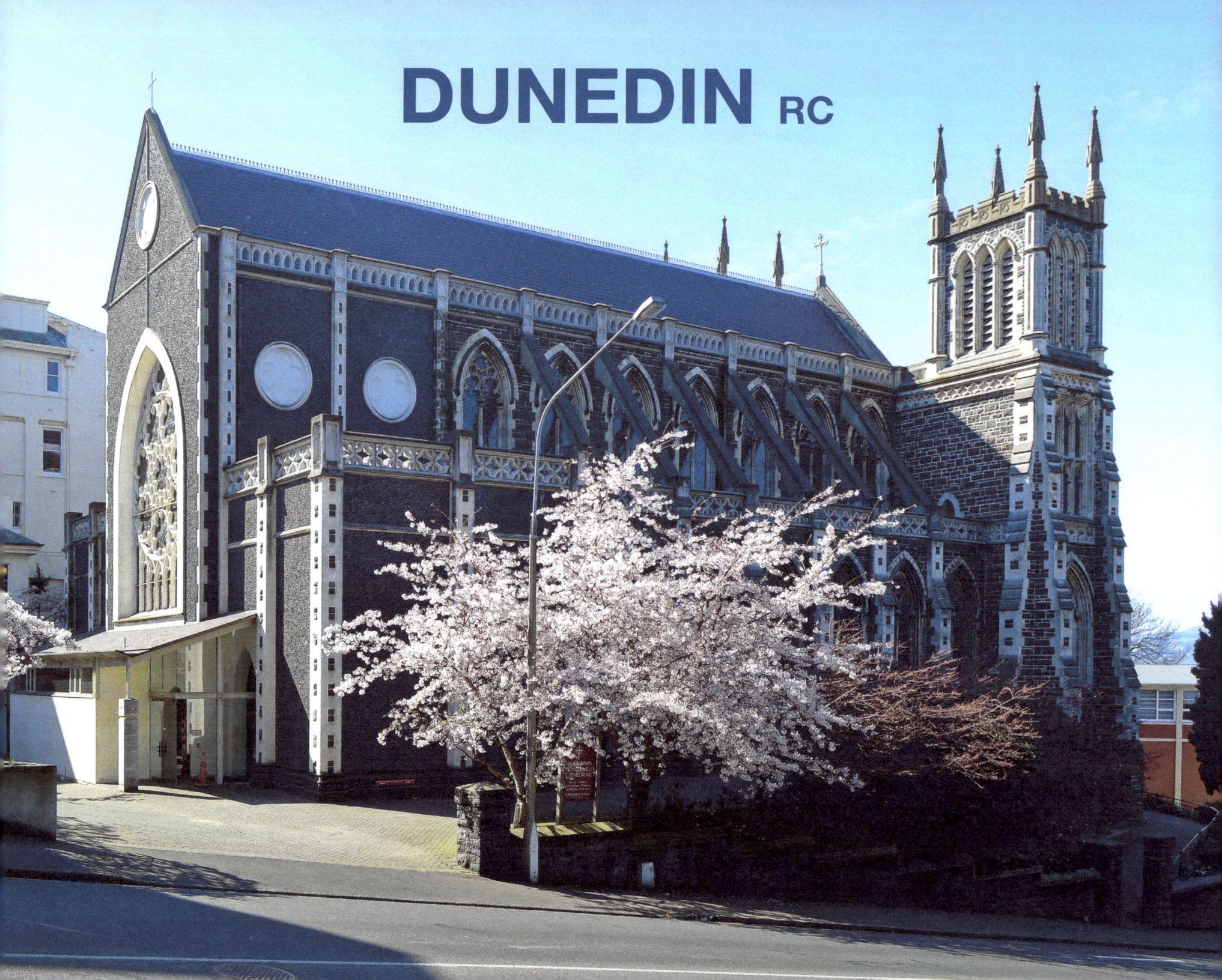

DUNEDIN RC

Nave windows

Unusual East rose window

▲ West nave and window above door ▼

St Joseph's Cathedral is the cathedral for the Roman Catholic Diocese of Dunedin. It is a Gothic revival cathedral designed by Francis Petre, and is located on City Rise, a short climb up from the city centre. It dates from 1886. An unusual feature is a beautiful chapel alongside and above the nave, accessed by an external flight of steps!

West wall

Side chapel altar

Station of cross

Side chapel: Holy Family

St Peter's is the Anglican Cathedral in Hamilton, located in the Waikato region. It is located on a small hill, known as Cathedral Hill. The present building was completed in 1916. It was modelled on a 15th-century church in Norfolk, England. The Cathedral has a ring of eight bells which were cast by the Mears & Stainbank foundry of Whitechapel, London.

Processional cross

Nave

Font

West window

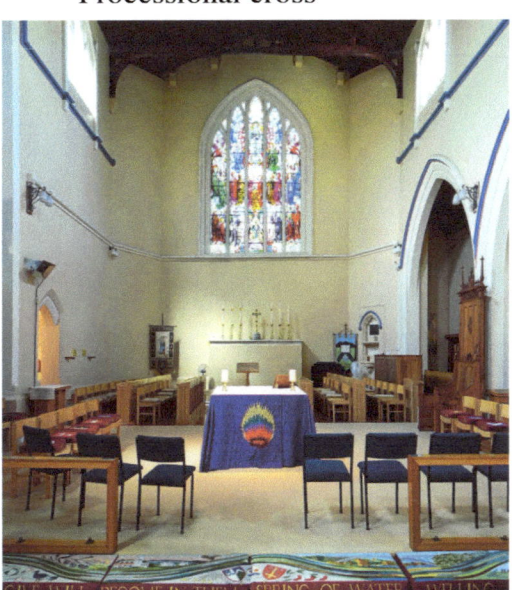
Sanctuary

Nave windows

Taonga

Kneelers

HAMILTON RC

Sacred Heart

North nave

South window panel

The Cathedral of the Blessed Virgin Mary is the cathedral of the Roman Catholic Diocese of Hamilton. It was opened in 1975, replacing an earlier neo-classical building known as St Mary's Church. The Cathedral of the Blessed Virgin Mary was dedicated and renamed in 1980 and rededicated, following refurbishment, in 2008. There are many rich colours to be found here, and many unexpected treasures – especially the large West window, 'The Resurrection of Christ', by Dutch immigrant artist Martin Roestenburg.

West window

Sanctuary altar

Memorial window

Our Lady shrine

NAPIER

Ruins of the old cathedral after the 1931 earthquake

Nave windows

Regimental colours

The Waiapu Cathedral of Saint John the Evangelist, Napier, is the Anglican Cathedral of the Diocese of Waiapu. Construction of the present building was completed in 1965, and the cathedral was consecrated in 1967. It is built in an Art Deco style, and replaces the previous brick Cathedral of St John which was destroyed in the 1931 Hawke's Bay earthquake.

Old window fragments

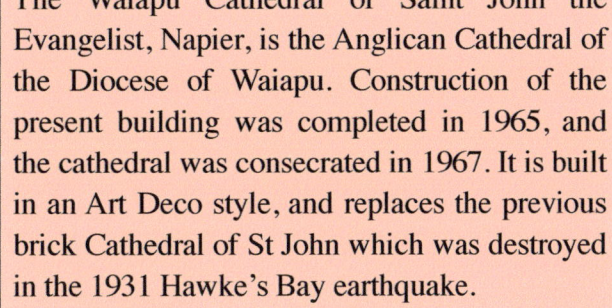
Some of the many nave icons

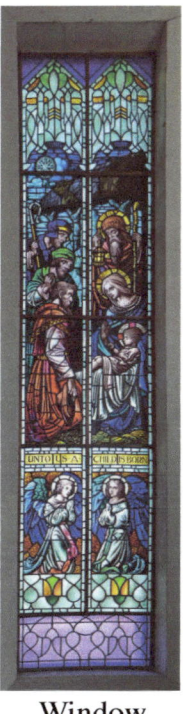
Window

Nave from balcony

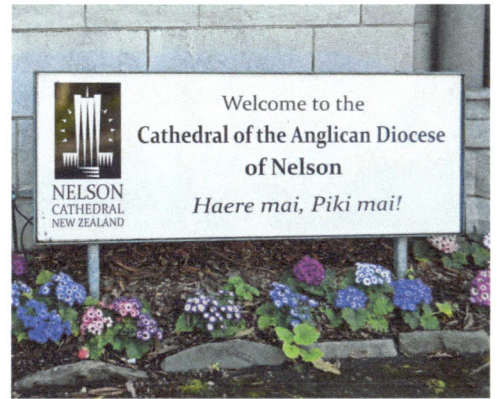
Welcome sign

Altar

Lectern

Organ

Bishop's crest

Christ Church Cathedral is an Anglican cathedral in Nelson; it is set on a hill in the city centre, surrounded by lush planting. The tower, which is 35 metres high, can be seen from afar. Construction of the current church began in 1925 and was completed in 1965. The majority of marble was sourced from the nearby Pakikiruna Range, and was to be used in blocks. But after the 1929 Murchison earthquake it was decided to grind the marble down and mix it with plaster.

Font

Nave window

Nave

Transept wheel window

NEW PLYMOUTH

Baptismal panels

Bell

Cathedra

Māori memorial

The Taranaki Cathedral Church of St Mary (formerly known as St Mary's Church) is the oldest stone church in New Zealand, and at the same time one of the newest cathedrals in the Anglican Communion. The original church, was built between 1845 and 1846 in the Gothic Revival style. It was designed by Frederick Thatcher, a London-trained architect, one of the first settlers in New Plymouth.

Double nave

North transept

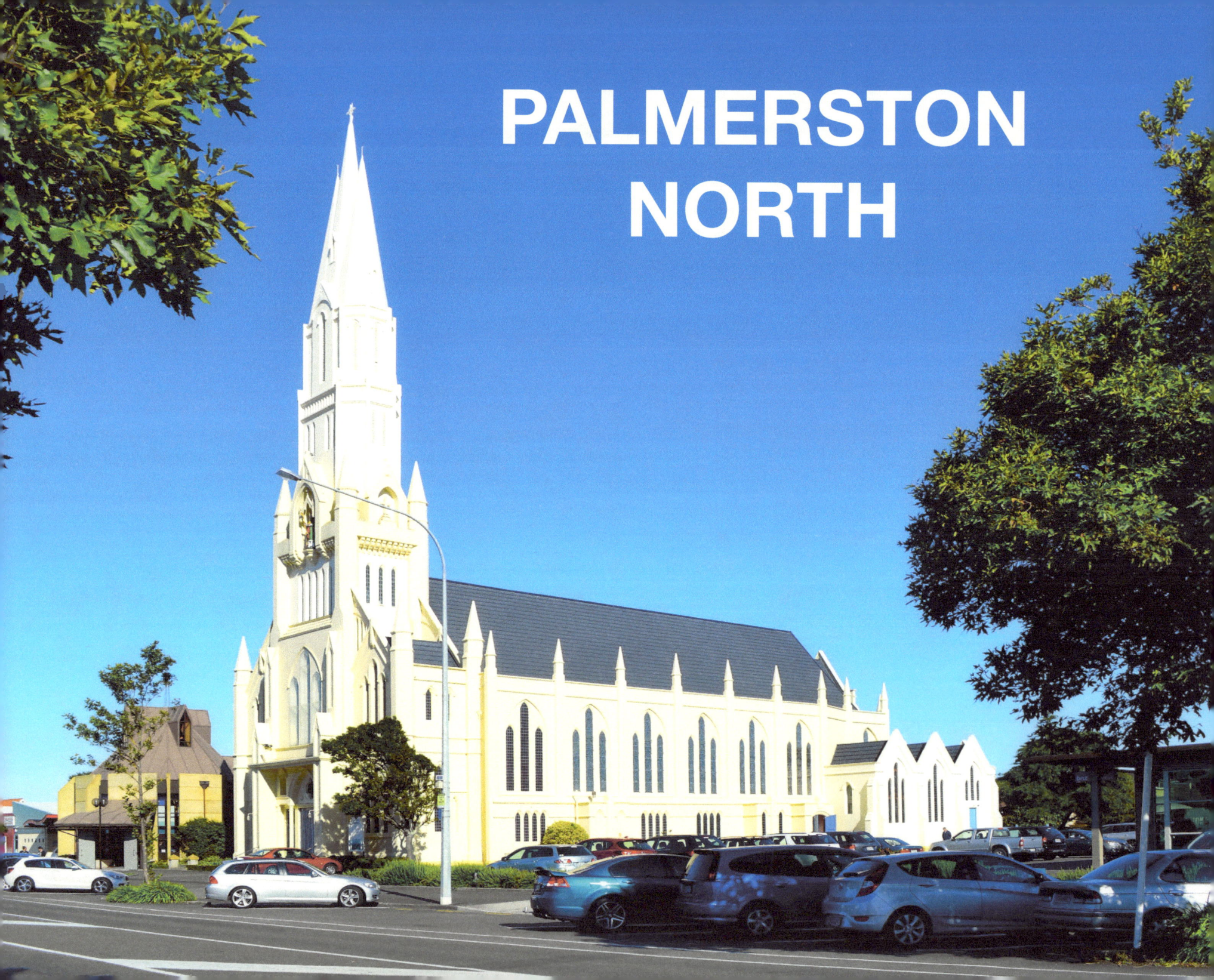

North nave windows

Carvings on pew ends

Nave

The Cathedral of the Holy Spirit is the Gothic Revival style cathedral of the Roman Catholic Diocese of Palmerston North. It opened in 1925 as St Patrick's Church and was rededicated to the Holy Spirit as the cathedral when the diocese was established in 1980. In 1988, the cathedral was renovated, expanded and reordered. The building was designed by the notable architect Frederick de Jersey Clere.

Spire

Māori Tiki

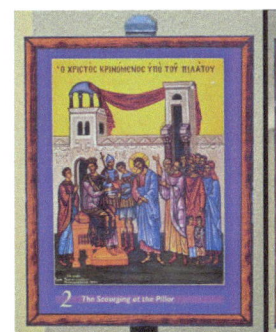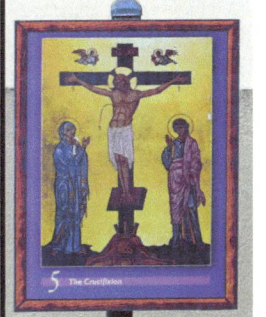
Mysteries

Altar with spectacular flame panels

OLD ST PAUL'S

Nave

Pulpit

Two minor transept windows

Old St Paul's (formerly St Paul's Pro-Cathedral) is a historic site and a wedding venue in the heart of Wellington. The building served as the parish church of Thorndon and the pro-cathedral of the Anglican Diocese of Wellington between 1866 and 1964. It was built in 19th-century Gothic Revival architectural style.

Font

North nave windows

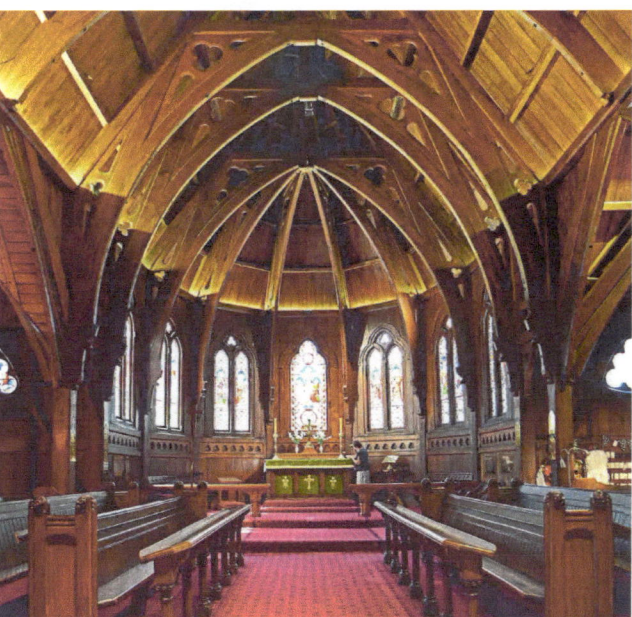
Sanctuary apse

Nave

Sashes

St Paul's Cathedral is an Anglican church in the city of Wellington. It is the mother church of the Diocese of Wellington. The building was designed in the 1930s by New Zealand architect Cecil Wood. Construction began in 1954, and was completed in 1998. It was constructed in reinforced concrete as a precaution against earthquakes. The building began to be used as an Anglican cathedral in 1964 (replacing Old St Paul's), and was consecrated in 2001.

Holm Window

Pulpit

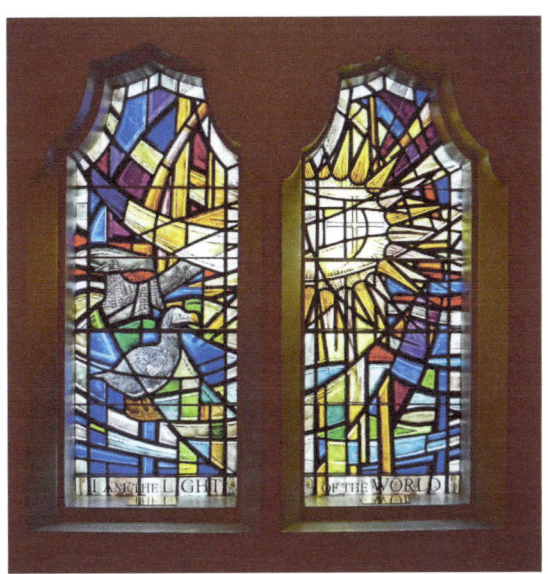
Ambulatory East window

Angels, candle, font

High altar and Dossal

Entry to the Blessed Sacrament Chapel

Angels

Font

Sculpture

Altar and 'Sacred Heart of Jesus' by Refto

The Metropolitan Cathedral of the Sacred Heart and of Saint Mary His Mother, better known as Sacred Heart Cathedral, is a Roman Catholic cathedral in Wellington. It is the parish church of the Thorndon Catholic parish (founded 1850) and the cathedral of the Archbishop of Wellington. The church was popularly known as 'the Basilica', because of its Palladian architectural style. It was designated as the cathedral of Wellington in 1984 after earthquake strengthening and a number of additions. The Cathedral has been recently closed for further seismic strengthening.

Windows in the Blessed Sacrament Chapel

GLOSSARY

Ambo : raised speaking stand

Apse : semicircular recess/extension

Aumbry : small cupboard/niche used to store sacred objects

Boss : ornamental covering of join of vaulting ribs

Capital : broader section of head of column

Cathedra : a bishop's official throne

Chancel : space reserved for clergy and choir

Chantry : endowment for priests to celebrate masses for soul of founder

Chapel : small worship space

Chapter House : building, usually round, where early monks read a daily chapter

Choir : space used by singing group (choir) and clergy

Clerestory : upper part of cathedral containing series of windows

Cloister : covered walk, typically with columns on one side around a quadrangle

Crossing : the intersection of nave and transepts

Font : receptacle for water used in baptism

Gothic : architectural style with characteristic pointed arches

Grisaille : monochrome painting, appearing in some windows

Icon : devotional painting on wood

Kneeler : cushion or bench for kneeling on

Lancet (window) : tall narrow window with pointed arch at top

Lantern : lamp; capped roof opening with glazed surround

Lectern : tall stand with sloping book rest on top

Misericord : supporting ledge on underside of hinged seat

Narthex : antechamber, large porch

Nave : rectangular space in cathedral where congregation sits

Norman : early architectural style with large columns and round arches

Pulpit : elevated platform used by preacher

Pulpitum : screen separating nave and choir

Quire : alternative spelling of choir; often used to denote choir seating

Reredos : ornamental screen behind the high altar

Romanesque : early architectural style with large columns and round arches

Rood : cross or crucifix high above entrance to chancel

Rose Window : circular window with tracery suggesting a rose

Sacristy : room where priest prepares for services

Sanctuary : most holy part of cathedral, usually East of chancel

Triforium : gallery or arcade above main arches and below clerestory

Vault : arched structure of masonry forming a ceiling or roof

Vestry : alternative word for sacristy

Wheel Window : circular window with 'spokes' out from the cemtre

www.ingramcontent.com/pod-product-compliance
Lightning Source LLC
Chambersburg PA
CBHW050851010526
44107CB00047BA/1575